D1736720

our
Environment

Ecotourism

Peggy J. Parks

KIDHAVEN PRESS
A part of Gale, Cengage Learning

GALE
CENGAGE Learning

Detroit • New York • San Francisco • New Haven, Conn • Waterville, Maine • London

© 2006 Gale, Cengage Learning

For more information, contact
KidHaven Press
27500 Drake Rd.
Farmington Hills, MI 48331-3535
Or you can visit our Internet site at gale.cengage.com

Photo credits: Cover: © Brian A. Vikander/CORBIS; AFP/Getty Images, 10, 24, 39; B. & C. Alexander/Photo Researchers, Inc., 29; © Brian A. Vikander/CORBIS, 9; Getty Images, 20; © Hal Beral/CORBIS, 35; © Jeremy Horner/CORBIS, 21; © Martin Harvey/CORBIS, 28; © Mason Florence/Lonely Planet Images, 6; Maury Aaseng, 32–33; National Geographic/Getty Images, 12, 26; © Nik Wheeler/CORBIS, 17, 18; © Shannon Nace/Lonely Planet Images, 15; © Stephen Saks/Lonely Planet Images, 5; Tim Graham/Getty Images, 37

LIBRARY OF CONGRESS CATALOGING-IN-PUBLICATION DATA

Parks, Peggy J., 1951–
  Ecotourism / by Peggy J. Parks.
      p. cm. — (Our environment)
  Includes bibliographical references and index.
  ISBN 0-7377-3048-X (hard cover : alk. paper)
  1. Ecotourism—Juvenile literature. I. Title. II. Series.
  G156.5.E26P37 2005
  338.4'791—dc22

Printed in the United States of America
  5 6 7 12 11 10 09 08

contents

chapter one

Nature in Peril

Earth is filled with nature's works of art. There are lush rain forests, pristine tropical beaches, wooded mountain ranges, and majestic glaciers. These natural wonders have survived for ages, so it is hard to imagine that they could ever be destroyed. Yet many of them are endangered.

The causes are many. The growing popularity of tourism in the world's wilderness areas is one threat. Large numbers of tourists visiting rain forests and other fragile areas can strain delicate **ecosystems**. Another threat comes from governments and native peoples. In an effort to earn money, they sometimes damage or destroy natural areas.

Tourism as a Solution

Environmental organizations worldwide are concerned about the serious risks to nature and wildlife.

A group of tourists in Costa Rica learns about the country's wildlife during an ecotour along a river.

A guide in Japan teaches an ecotourist about mangrove trees and the ecosystem they live in.

Many believe **ecotourism** can go a long way toward solving problems in wilderness areas. Ecotourism is defined by the International Ecotourism Society (TIES) as "responsible travel to natural areas that conserves the environment and improves the well-being of local people."[1]

Through ecotourism, people can experience nature and wildlife without causing harm. They often will take part in activities that help protect both. Local communities are also supposed to benefit from ecotourism. People living near tropical rain forests, for example, sometimes cut down trees to clear land for farming. But rain forest soil often lacks nutrients that make for good farmland. In the end, rain forests are ruined, and local people earn little money from their efforts. Ecotourism provides a way for them to earn money from tourism and avoids destruction of precious natural resources and wildlife.

The Roots of Ecotourism

Although worldwide awareness of ecotourism has increased in recent years, it is not a new idea. It was born in the late 1970s, when the negative effects of tourism were first becoming obvious. A Mexican architect and environmentalist named Héctor Ceballos-Lascuráin was one of the first to use the term "ecotourism." He led a conservation group that was working to protect wetlands in the Yucatán Peninsula in Mexico. Tourism was harming the wetlands and other fragile ecosystems, and the group was concerned.

Ceballos-Lascuráin believed there was a way for tourism to benefit the environment and wildlife, rather than causing harm. He also saw ecotourism as a way to boost local economies and create jobs. He and others in his group began talking with tourism professionals, government officials, and others about this idea. As a result of their efforts, interest in ecotourism grew.

From Enemies to Partners

Another early supporter of ecotourism was Costas Christ of Conservation International. During the 1970s, Christ was working as a researcher in the East African country of Kenya, which was quickly becoming a popular tourist destination. One site that attracted many tourists was the Samburu Game Reserve, once home to the Samburu and Maasai peoples. When the government created this reserve, the Samburu and Maasai were forced to move to other areas. For centuries they had lived off the land, eating roots and bark, as well as vegetables they had grown. They raised livestock such as sheep, cattle, and goats. Theirs had been a simple, traditional way of life, and the loss of their land created many hardships for them.

At the same time, Kenya's national parks and wildlife reserves, including the Samburu Game Reserve, attracted thousands of visitors every day. But the Samburu and Maasai did not share in the wealth coming into the country as a result of this tourism. They became frustrated.

In 1978 a massive brush fire raced through the game reserve, burning everything in its path. Panicked animals tried to escape, and some died in the blaze. Christ joined lodge workers and park rangers in an effort to fight the fire, and they finally put it out. Afterwards, he learned that local people had set the fire. He began meeting with them to discuss their concerns. They told Christ they

Members of the Maasai and Samburu (pictured) were forced from their homelands when the Kenyan government created the Samburu Game Reserve in the 1970s.

hated the park because it had destroyed their way of life, as he explains: "They expressed anger at tourists who spent millions of dollars to visit Samburu Game Reserve while on safari and stay at the fancy lodges while the local people had no wells, no schools, no clinics, and struggled for basic needs. Why, they asked bitterly, should they support a park that left them worse off than before?"[2]

Christ began working with the communities and governmental organizations. He was convinced that the only way the reserve would succeed was if people living there had a stake in it. By 1994 the Kenya

A Maasai guide leads an ecotourist on a camel ride. Ecotourism benefits both the Maasai and Samburu peoples.

Wildlife Service had created new policies for the Samburu Game Reserve. The Samburu and Maasai peoples became partners in the venture. They were involved in making decisions about the park, and they shared in the profits. Instead of being threatened by tourism, they now viewed it as something beneficial for their way of life.

Saving the Rain Forest

Christ has also been involved in conservation efforts in Gabon, a country in western Africa. Gabon is home to some of the most magnificent natural beauty in the world. Tropical rain forests cover nearly 80,000 square miles (207,000 square kilometers), and the lush green canopy stretches all the way down to the Atlantic shore. Gabon is one of the few remaining places where tigers roam wild and free, gorillas and chimpanzees swing through the trees, and herds of elephants walk along the beach. Research scientist Michael Fay describes the area: "Blue seas, white sand, elephants, whales, sea turtles, monkeys, bush pigs, unbelievable scenery. Gabon has it all. It has everything that everyone ever dreams about in paradise."[3]

Until recently, Gabon's precious resources were being rapidly destroyed. Trees were cut down and sold to logging industries. Elephants were killed for their ivory, and many other animals were hunted for their meat and fur. There were laws in place to prevent these activities, but the Gabonese government was not enforcing them. The country needed the money from these activities too badly.

Conservation International, the Wildlife Conservation Society, and the World Wildlife Fund began working with government officials in Gabon. They introduced the idea of ecotourism as a way to help this very poor country make money. As a result of their efforts, in September 2002 the government agreed to create thirteen new national parks to protect millions of acres of rain forest. These parks would bring in money without destroying the country's natural resources. Today, even though all Gabon's problems are not yet solved, Christ says that ecotourism has made a positive difference.

Environmental Wear and Tear

Ecotourism has also been hailed as the solution to another problem—the massive growth of tourism. Growing numbers of people are traveling to the world's remote, pristine areas. Nature lovers are drawn to the spectacular beauty of Earth's oceans, mountains, deserts, and other scenic areas. As a result, nature travel has become the fastest-growing type of tourism—and this growth has led to a number of serious problems. The ever-growing numbers of tourists place great strain on the natural wonders that drew them to the areas in the first place.

Ecotourists from all over the world travel to the rain forests of Gabon to see magnificent animals like this gorilla.

Conservation International and the United Nations Environmental Programme (UNEP) found this to be the case in a 2001 study. They identified places throughout the world where tourism has grown at staggering rates. Two examples are the Asian nations of Laos and Cambodia. Between 1990 and 2000, tourism in these countries increased by more than 2,000 percent. During the same period, Vietnam's tourism jumped by 1,000 percent. Sharp increases were also seen in South Africa and countries in South America.

The study showed that an increase in tourism has caused significant damage to fragile ecosystems such as rain forests, mountains, and coastal areas. UNEP, TIES, and other such organizations believe that ecotourism could help prevent this damage. TIES founder Megan Epler Wood explains: "Tourism has a tendency to become something like a steamroller wherever it goes. It can completely destroy natural places. Ecotourism is about trying to stop that."[4]

Hope for the Future

From lush tropical rain forests to towering mountain ranges, Earth is filled with natural beauty. Yet because of human activities, nature and wildlife are at risk of being destroyed. Environmental organizations and conservationists are concerned about the damage being done, but they believe there is hope for the future—and that hope lies in ecotourism.

chapter two

Tourism with a Conscience

Interest in ecotourism continues to grow. TIES, for instance, has become an international network of environmental groups, governments, tourism professionals, and other organizations. Its mission is to uphold and support sound ecotourism principles. TIES develops guidelines and standards, conducts research, and provides education and training for tourism professionals. The group also produces materials that help inform the public about ecotourism and its many benefits.

Tropical Rain Forests

One group that is active in this movement is Rainforest Expeditions in Peru. Its goal is for people throughout the world to learn about the Amazon rain forests of South America, including how they are threatened. In 1996 Rainforest

A guide in Peru prepares to lead a group of ecotourists on a boat expedition along the Amazon River.

Expeditions formed a partnership with the Native Community of Infierno, a group of people living near the Tambopata River. The people of this community depended on the rain forest for food, medicine, and shelter, but they also needed to earn money. One solution was to cut down trees so the land could be used for farming and raising live-stock. However, they wanted to preserve the rain forest, rather than destroy it.

Rainforest Expeditions offered a solution. The group would build a tourist lodge in the rain forest called Posada Amazonas. Local people could work there in various jobs, such as providing guided tours for guests. They would be able to preserve their natural environment and receive a portion of the profits generated by the lodge. They agreed, and the two groups signed a partnership agreement.

Today, Posada Amazonas is well known and highly respected as an ecotourism operation. The lodge was built from local materials, so it blends in with the natural surroundings. Guests who stay at Posada Amazonas participate in nature walks and canoe trips that are guided by local people. They learn about the rain forest's unique vegetation and wildlife, as well as local culture. Ecotourists leave with a renewed appreciation for tropical rain forests and why they should be protected, and the money they spend during their stay helps to support the community and their way of life.

Ecotourism in Africa

Another highly respected ecotourism group is Conservation Corporation Africa, or CC Africa. The group operates 37 safari camps in six African countries. All of the camps are dedicated to preserving the natural environment and benefiting local communities. Four camps are located in CC Africa's Phinda Private Game Reserve in South Africa. The enormous reserve covers 42,000 acres (17,000 hectares) of land. Before it was created,

Ecotourists in a Jeep marvel at a herd of giraffes roaming along the savanna of the Phinda Private Game Reserve in South Africa.

years of farming and cattle grazing had left the land scarred and barren. With the help of ecologists and wildlife experts, CC Africa was able to restore the land. Nearly 2,000 wild animals, including lions, leopards, rhinos, elephants, and giraffes, were moved there from other areas. The animals began to thrive, and have since tripled in number.

Guests who stay at Phinda can participate in wild-game safaris. They are accompanied by trained local guides, who take them to areas where

A chef at the Phinda Private Game Reserve serves breakfast to ecotourists on safari.

wild game live. During the journeys, tourists search for animal tracks and learn how to identify various creatures. They also learn about the local environment, folklore, and native culture.

Phinda has provided enormous benefits to the native peoples who live in the area. CC Africa provided training and jobs as guides or other workers at the reserve. The organization also used tourism profits to set up a special fund known as the Rural Investment Fund, which provides money for schools, health care clinics, and other community needs. The fund also assists those who want to start small businesses. For example, money from the fund helped build a market where native women could sell handmade beadwork and baskets. Because of the numerous ways Phinda has benefited nature, wildlife, and the South African people, it is often called an ecotourism success story.

The Shompole Community Ecotourism Development Project in Kenya is another successful ecotourism venture. In the late 1970s, the Maasai who lived in Shompole were very poor. They needed to find a way to support themselves. With the financial help of an organization known as the African Conservation Centre, the Maasai built a stunning tourist lodge. They named the lodge Maaoleng, meaning "completely Maasai." The income from tourism goes directly into a fund that is used to benefit the local community. According to Costas Christ, the Shompole project "is a great example of ecotourism in action—where conservation and local people benefit together."[5]

Research Ecotourists

Phinda and Shompole are examples of one kind of ecotourism. There are other types of ecotourism as well, such as trips that involve people in scientific research. The goal of these ecotours is the same: to preserve the environment and wildlife while helping local communities.

One example is Biosphere Expeditions, which takes people to exotic locations all over the world. Biosphere projects usually involve studies of wild

The African Conservation Centre has taught many of the poorer members of the Maasai, like this mother and child, to support themselves through ecotourism.

A Biosphere Expeditions study in Sri Lanka is working to teach local farmers how to live in harmony with elephant populations.

animal populations. Some of these studies are aimed at helping local people find ways to live side-by-side with animals so that neither the people nor the animals are threatened.

In one Biosphere expedition, participants traveled to the island of Sri Lanka to study endangered elephants. Hundreds of elephants live in the island's Wasgamuwa National Park. In recent years, Sri Lankan farmers have killed as many as 150 elephants annually because the creatures are very destructive. They wander out of the park at night, eating and trampling crops. The farmers, who earn a living from their crops, cannot feed their families when this happens.

Biosphere understands the difficulties faced by the farmers, but the group also wants to help protect the elephants. Scientists and volunteers visit local villages and farms to interview people about the damage to crops. They survey the forests, jungles, and grassy plains within and around the park to watch how the elephants behave. Sometimes participants spend the night in tree huts, waiting for elephants to appear at watering holes. Then they record the creatures' behaviors and movements.

Biosphere's goal for this research is to learn why the elephants are seeking food from the farmland, rather than finding it in the park. When the project is finished, scientists hope to have enough information to make specific recommendations to Sri Lankan officials. They want to resolve the conflict between humans and elephants so that both can survive.

Vacations with a Purpose

Ecotourism revolves around nature and wildlife, but ecotours are much more than just vacations. Whether travelers visit rain forests in Peru or perform research in Sri Lanka, they gain a great deal from the experience. They have a renewed appreciation for nature and wildlife, and the money they spend helps support the people in local communities.

chapter three

"Something Weird Is Happening in the Wilderness"

Ecotourism can benefit both people and wildlife. It does not always bring benefits, however. Sometimes these well-intentioned programs do more harm than good. For one thing, more people traveling to the world's scenic places means more strain on the natural environment. It also means more dangers for animals in the wild. Environmental journalist Anil Ananthaswamy warns of this when he says, "Something weird is happening in the wilderness. The animals are becoming restless. Polar bears and penguins, dolphins and dingoes, even birds in the rain forest are becoming stressed. . . . The cause is a pursuit intended to have the opposite effect: ecotourism."[6]

Ecotourism vs. Greenwashing

Ecotourism should not cause such problems. Reputable ecotourism groups are very careful about their facilities and trips. They hire knowledgeable, trained guides and strictly limit the number of people who are allowed in a particular area. These guides are also mindful of keeping enough distance between humans and wildlife. So how is it possible for ecotourism to be harmful?

Much of the problem is that the word "ecotourism" is overused. Tempted by opportunities to make money, growing numbers of tourism companies describe their trips as "ecotours" even though they are not. This practice is referred to as **green-**

German ecotourists snap photos as a member of their group reaches out to touch a giant Galápagos turtle.

washing, or ecotourism lite. The trips may involve trekking up a mountain, taking a whale-watching cruise, or viewing wild animals in the jungle. While these are definitely nature trips, they do not necessarily benefit the environment, wildlife, or people. Costas Christ explains: "Too often people confuse nature tourism . . . with ecotourism. They are not the same thing. Ecotourism is directly linked to conserving nature and bringing benefits to local people."[7]

Jungle Animals

Christ has been involved in many ecotourism projects in Africa and elsewhere in the world. The World Trade Organization says Africa is one of the fastest-growing destinations for international tourists. This is especially true in South Africa. More than 6.7 million people visited the country in 2004. Tourists flock to the African continent to admire the breathtaking scenery and exotic wild animals. They travel on safaris where they can see lions, tigers, elephants, giraffes, and other creatures in their natural environment.

According to Conservation International, large numbers of visitors to African jungles have contributed to the dwindling population of cheetahs. These magnificent spotted creatures are the fastest land mammals on Earth. In order to survive, cheetahs must kill and eat natural prey. They hunt hoofed mammals such as gazelles and wildebeests.

A cheetah walks past a herd of wildebeests in Kenya. Sadly, ecotourism in the African jungle has contributed to the dwindling population of cheetahs.

However, groups of tourists become fascinated when they see cheetahs racing after and catching their prey. Curious people move close to the creatures to watch them eat. The cheetahs become frightened and run away, leaving their hard-won kill behind. Hyenas and other scavenger animals move in to take the food away, and the cheetahs and their cubs are left without food.

Making Animals Sick

Just as ecotourism has influenced the animals' behavior, it has also affected their health. Wildlife can catch diseases from humans. Germs and bacteria are carried in mud and dirt that cling to clothing, gear, and vehicles, as well as in sewage. When creatures come into contact with these germs and bacteria, they can become sick.

One such incident occurred in a national park in the African country of Uganda. Uganda is home to hundreds of wild mountain gorillas. The gorillas are curious creatures, and sometimes they leave the forest to search for food in areas where humans camp. The gorillas pick up and examine pieces of clothing or bedding that campers leave behind. In 2000, tiny mites living in the fabrics infected some of the gorillas with a skin disease known as **mange**. This caused patches of their fur to fall out, and made their skin sore, flaky, and itchy. Although mange is rarely life-threatening, scientists worry that the gorillas could catch other types of human diseases such as measles. If that happened, the consequences could be devastating to the gorilla population. Guy Cowlishaw, a conservation researcher from England, says that tourists have a responsibility to prevent exposing animals to disease: "It's important that groups are kept small, and distances between humans and gorillas are strictly maintained."[8]

Another outbreak of disease occurred in the African country of Botswana—but this one was much more deadly. In 2002 researchers reported that mongooses and small, burrowing mammals known as meerkats were infected with tuberculosis. Because it is a human disease, scientists knew

Tourists photograph a male mountain gorilla in the Congo. Wildlife can sometimes catch diseases like mange from such close human contact.

the animals had been infected by tourists who were carrying tuberculosis germs. By getting too close to wildlife, the tourists' germs had spread. Many of the animals became very sick, and a large number of meerkats living in Botswana's Kalahari Desert died from the disease.

Effects on Polar Animals

As ecotourism continues to grow more popular, scientists fear that the world's wildlife will be in even greater danger from human germs and diseases. One area of particular concern is Antarctica. Currently about 130 cruises visit Antarctica each year, carrying a total of 12,000 to 14,000 people. This is a small number compared to other tourist destinations. However, more and more people are choosing to travel to Antarctica, which means the risk to animals will likely increase.

Scientists are already concerned about the mysterious deaths of thousands of Antarctic animals, including crabeater seals, penguin chicks, and sea lions. No one is sure what caused the deaths, but scientists suspect it was human bacteria or viruses. Australian scientist Knowles Kerry, an expert on Antarctica, expresses his concern about this risk: "We need to be vigilant, to limit the possibility of human activity introducing disease into Antarctica's wildlife."[9]

Ecotourists paddle kayaks along a frigid peninsula in Antarctica. Some scientists worry that Antarctic ecosystems are at risk from the adverse effects of ecotourism.

Nature at Risk

Some scientists fear that habitats are also at risk from the popularity of ecotourism. They worry about harm to fragile and sensitive areas in forests, wetlands, and other ecosystems. Where there are large numbers of tourists, construction of roads, lodges, and other tourist facilities usually also follows. It can be difficult to add these structures without harming habitat.

According to the environmental group Mountain Partnership, the risk is especially great for Earth's mountains. A rich variety of plant and animal life can be found in many mountain areas. When these areas are developed for tourists, ecosystems can be thrown out of balance, threatening plants and animals. Also, many people live in mountainous areas and increased tourism could threaten their way of life. Mountain Partnership says the secret of balancing the needs of mountain people and tourism lies in careful planning. Local people must be closely involved in decision making, as well as being able to benefit from money spent by tourists.

Ecotourism was designed to be a positive force for nature, wildlife, and people. However, not all nature vacations are truly ecotours. Also, as the demand for ecotourism continues to grow, this could strain fragile ecosystems and put wildlife at risk. If that happens, the very activity that was intended to protect nature and the environment could instead cause harm.

chapter Four

Ecotourism Today and Tomorrow

While there are drawbacks to ecotourism, it has many supporters. They believe it has potential for being good both for the environment and for peoples around the world. Mountain Partnership states on its Web site: "Handled properly, ecotourism can be a valuable tool in advancing tourism, especially for poor . . . communities in the developing world, without destroying natural resources and the environment."[10]

An Ecotourism Village

Some areas of the world are proof of how carefully managed ecotourism can protect and preserve nature and help local communities. One example is on the island of Atauro, which is off the coast of Indonesia. Atauro is a land of lush rain forests,

Ecotourism Hot Spots Worldwide

NORTH
AMERICA

SOUTH
AMERICA

1. Mexico
2. Guatemala
3. Belize
4. Honduras
5. Costa Rica
6. Panama
7. Dominican
Republic
8. Jamaica
9. Colombia
10. Venezuela
11. Ecuador
12. Peru
13. Brazil
14. Bolivia
15. Chile

Source: World Tourism Organization (Tourism Marketing Trends) Conservation International, 2003.

ASIA

EUROPE

AFRICA

26

25

24

27

28

16

17

18

20 19

22 21

23

30

29

31

AUSTRALIA

32

33

ANTARCTICA

34

16. Kenya	21. Botswana	26. China	31. New Guinea
17. Tanzania	22. Namibia	27. Thailand	32. Australia
18. Malawi	23. South Africa	28. Sri Lanka	33. New Zealand
19. Mozambique	24. India	29. Indonesia	34. Antarctica
20. Zimbabwe	25. Nepal	30. Philippines	

high mountain cliffs, tropical beaches, and spectac-ular coral reefs. In the late 1990s, people from other parts of the world began to visit Atauro. Many of them expressed a desire to build resorts that would attract wealthy tourists. The local people knew that tourism could generate much-needed income, but they were fearful of letting outsiders control the development. Australian educator Gabrielle Samson, who lives on Atauro, explains: "There was talk of casinos and resorts and the potential of lots of cash. These people are very vulnerable. It's their land, they own it and they are quite poor."[11] Samson held workshops with leaders from the community to discuss what they would like to do. They said they were interested in attracting tourists. However, they did not want tourism to spoil the natural beauty of their island. So, they decided to build their own ecotourism village.

The village is called Tua Koin. It consists of eight thatched-roof cabins that overlook the Timor Sea. Local tradespeople designed the village to blend in with the environment, using natural materials such as bamboo and local timber to build the cabins. Solar energy provides power for lighting at night, and water comes from a mountain spring. There are facilities for recycling water and trash.

Tua Koin has been called a model ecotourism operation. Local people work at the village and earn money for their services. The profits generat-ed by tourism have also paid for medical clinics, schools, and other community projects. Samson hopes that resorts throughout the world will copy what was done on the island of Atauro.

Ecotourism in a Rain Forest

Another example of model ecotourism is in the Brazilian village of Alta Floresta. A businesswoman

The ecotourism village of Alta Floresta in Brazil was established to help protect indigenous wildlife like these Jabiru storks and to slow deforestation.

and conservationist named Vitória da Riva Carvalho built an ecotourism lodge and research center in the Amazon rain forest. People living in this area had been cutting down trees in the forest to clear land for farming. Riva Carvalho wanted to preserve the forest, and thought she could do so through ecotourism. When she presented her idea to the local people, she got little support. They assumed she only wanted to make money off the forest. Little by little, Riva Carvalho convinced the natives of her sincere desire to save the forest. She also showed them how they could benefit from preserving it. Today, local people work in the ecotourism lodge. They also work as tour guides and in the research center. Alta Floresta is successful and is embraced by the community. Riva Carvalho explains: "They see that I am working for the community, and that we can all benefit from protecting the forest. One of the most beautiful ways to protect nature is through ecotourism."[12]

Island Paradise

Ecotourism has also been positive for the Galápagos Islands. This is a chain of 120 volcanic islands in the Pacific Ocean about 600 miles (965 kilometers) off the coast of Ecuador. The Galápagos Islands have one of the most unique ecosystems in the world. Giant tortoises live there, as do marine iguanas, tropical penguins, sea lions, and a large variety of rare birds. Many of the

A land iguana on the Galápagos Islands hunts for food among the cacti. The Galápagos Islands are home to one of the world's most unique ecosystems.

islands' creatures, plants, and flowers are found nowhere else on Earth.

According to environmental author Martha Honey, sound ecotourism practices have done much to protect the Galápagos Islands. She explains: "Tour operators, naturalist guides, national park officials, and research station scientists have worked together for decades to create a model for low-impact, high-quality ecotourism."[13]

Ecuador's government also plays a major role in protecting the Galápagos Islands. More than 95 percent of the land area is designated a national park. There is also a large protected marine reserve.

Tourism is strictly controlled, with most of the islands off-limits to tourists. In the areas where visitors are allowed, groups are restricted to a maximum of sixteen people. They must stay on designated paths and are accompanied by a guide at all times.

The Downside

But even though legislation and sound ecotourism practices have done much to protect the Galápagos Islands, their fragile ecosystem is still threatened. People throughout the world have discovered this beautiful and pristine area, leading to a sharp rise in tourism. In 1980 an estimated 17,500 people visited the islands. According to the World Wildlife Fund (WWF), that number has grown to more than 75,000 visitors each year. This has led to environmental damage such as trampling of vegetation and soil erosion, and has created problems with waste and pollution. Also, the number of tourist boats continues to rise. Some of these boats have been caught dumping kitchen waste, sewage, and used oil into the ocean waters.

The WWF says the most serious threat to the Galápagos Islands is from nonnative species, sometimes called **alien invasives**. These are organisms such as plants, bacteria, fungi, and insects. They were carried onto the islands by boats and airplanes, as well as humans, and now they threaten the existence of native species. Former park superintendent Arturo Izurieta expressed his concern about this: "We are fighting very hard against introduced organisms which are arriving probably every day without us knowing it. . . . The responsibility of preserving the ecosystems as they were

Nonnative species of plants, bacteria, fungi, and insects have been brought to the Galápagos Islands by tour boats and airplanes.

formed millions of years ago is one of my greatest concerns."[14]

The WWF calls the Galápagos Islands "a living paradise" and says its future is threatened by tourism. Although the organization supports ecotourism, it stresses that there are fragile areas of the Earth where even ecotourism could be harmful. WWF's Justin Woolford says the future of ecotourism will ultimately depend on travelers. If travelers support and insist on responsible tourism, travel organizations will be more likely to follow sound ecotourism practices.

A Worthwhile Effort

People who are committed to ecotourism know that it cannot eliminate all threats to nature and wildlife. But it has already made a positive difference in many parts of the world, and can continue to do so in other areas. Conservation International's Russell Mittermeier says worldwide adoption of ecotourism principles will be challenging. He also believes, however, there are enormous opportunities as more travelers are able to see and experience the wonders of nature. He observes: "What better way for people to properly appreciate Earth's biological splendor, the traditional cultures it supports and the importance of preserving both."[15]

Notes

Chapter 1: Nature in Peril

1. The International Ecotourism Society. www.eco tourism.org/index2.php?what-is-ecotourism.

2. Costas Christ, "Costas Christ, Conservation International," *Grist Magazine*, March 18, 2002. www. grist.org/comments/dispatches/2002/03/18/costas/index.html.

3. Quoted in John Nielsen, "Gabon Moves to Preserve Rainforests," National Public Radio (NPR), September 4, 2002. www.npr.org/programs/atc/features/2002/sept/gabon.

4. Quoted in Suhrid Sankar Chattopadhyay, "Towards Responsible Tourism," *Frontline*, February 16–March 1, 2002. www.frontlineonnet.com/fl1904/19040830.htm.

Chapter 2: Tourism with a Conscience

5. Christ, "Costas Christ, Conservation International."

Chapter 3: "Something Weird Is Happening in the Wilderness"

6. Anil Ananthaswamy, "Beware the Ecotourist: Nature Tourism Is a Valuable Growth Industry, but It

Has Far-Reaching Effects on the Wildlife It Relies On," *New Scientist*, March 6, 2004.

7. Christ, "Costas Christ, Conservation International."

8. Quoted in John Whitfield, "Humans Get Under Apes' Skin," *News@Nature.com*, September 4, 2001. www.nature.com/news/2001/010906/pf/010906-5 _pf.html.

9. Quoted in Ananthaswamy, "Beware the Ecotourist."

Chapter 4: Ecotourism Today and Tomorrow

10. "Mountains and Tourism—A Precarious Balance," Mountain Partnership, 2002. www.mountainpartner ship.org/themes/i-tourism02.html

11. Quoted in Tom Noble, "Ethical Tourism on an Untouched Island," *The Sun-Herald*, April 17, 2005. www.smh.com.au/news/Asia/Ethical-tourism-on-an-untouched-island/2005/04/16/1113509964786.html.

12. Quoted in Roger Hamilton, "A Businesswoman with a Mission," *IDB America*, February 2002. www.iadb. org/idbamerica/English/FEB02E/feb02e2-c.html.

13. Martha Honey, *Ecotourism and Sustainable Development: Who Owns Paradise?* Washington, DC: Island Press, 1999, p. 123.

14. Quoted in Honey, *Ecotourism and Sustainable Development,* p. 114.

15. Russell A. Mittermeier, "The Promise of Ecotourism," *Conservation Frontlines Online*, March 22, 2005. www. conservation.org/xp/frontlines/outlook/outlook 32.xml.

Glossary

alien invasives: Organisms such as plants, bacteria, fungi, and insects that are introduced to a particular area where they are not native.

ecosystems: Communities of living organisms (such as plants and animals) and the environments in which they live.

ecotourism: Responsible travel to natural areas that conserves the environment and improves the well-being of local people (as defined by the International Ecotourism Society).

greenwashing: The practice of selling a trip as an ecotour when it does not fit the criteria of ecotourism (also called ecotourism lite).

mange: A skin disease that infects furry animals such as gorillas.

For Further Exploration

Books

Christina M. Allen, *Hippos in the Night: Autobiographical Adventures in Africa.* New York: HarperCollins, 2003. The firsthand account of a young biologist who spent five weeks in the African countries of Kenya and Tanzania. She describes what she learned about the environment and wildlife, as well as the local peoples whose way of life is disappearing rapidly.

Yann Arthus-Bertrand, *The Future of the Earth: An Introduction to Sustainable Development for Young Readers.* New York: Harry N. Abrams, 2004. This book explains how human activities have changed the world and harmed forests, coastlines, coral reefs, and other natural wonders.

Rob Bowden, *Sustainable World: Environments.* San Diego: KidHaven, 2003. Explores human effects on the natural environment, including how damage to ecosystems is being balanced with positive efforts such as ecotourism.

Cristina Kessler, *All the King's Animals: The Return of Endangered Wildlife to Swaziland.* Honesville, PA: Boyds Mills, 2001. The true story of the African kingdom of Swaziland, which lost virtually all of its wildlife due to disease and poaching. Because of a conservationist named Ted Reilly, the land was once again brought to life. The book is enhanced by color photographs.

Periodicals

Denise Baldetti, "Across the African Savannah," *Crinkles*, January/February 2002.

Sean Price, "Saving Arctic Wildlife," *Junior Scholastic*, January 27, 1995.

Science Made Simple, "What Is the Environment? Why Is It Important? " April 2004.

Web Sites

Amazon Interactive (www.eduweb.com/amazon. html). An educational Web site designed to teach young people about the Amazon rain forests, including where they are, how rainy they are, and the people who live there. The site has an interactive game that allows kids to plan and manage their own ecotourism project.

Conservation International (www.conservation. org). An informative and interesting site with information about Earth's ecosystems and its many living creatures.

National Geographic Kids (www.nationalgeographic. com/kids). Includes many articles, activities, and projects designed to help young people better understand the environment and wildlife.

Index

About the Author

Peggy J. Parks holds a bachelor of science degree from Aquinas College in Grand Rapids, Michigan, where she graduated magna cum laude. An avid environmentalist and nature lover, Parks has written more than 40 books for Thomson Gale's KidHaven Press, Blackbirch Press, and Lucent Books imprints. She lives in Muskegon, Michigan, a town she says inspires her writing because of its location on the shores of Lake Michigan.